CORNERSTONES
for
Writing

Pupil's Book
Year 2

Leonie Bennett
Chris Buckton

Consultant
Alison Green

Series Editor
Jean Glasberg

CAMBRIDGE
UNIVERSITY PRESS

Five steps to

GOOD WRITING

1 **Modelling:** use a model text to help you learn how to write your own text

Use the activities in this book

2 **Plan your own text**

Use the planning frames or the activities in this book

3 **Draft your text**

Work on your own text

4 **Revise and edit your text**

Work on your own text

5 **Publish your text**

Work on your own text

 When you see this symbol, do this activity with a partner or in a group.

 When you see this symbol, practise saying out loud what you are going to write.

CONTENTS

How to write

a story with a familiar setting

1 Starting points for a story

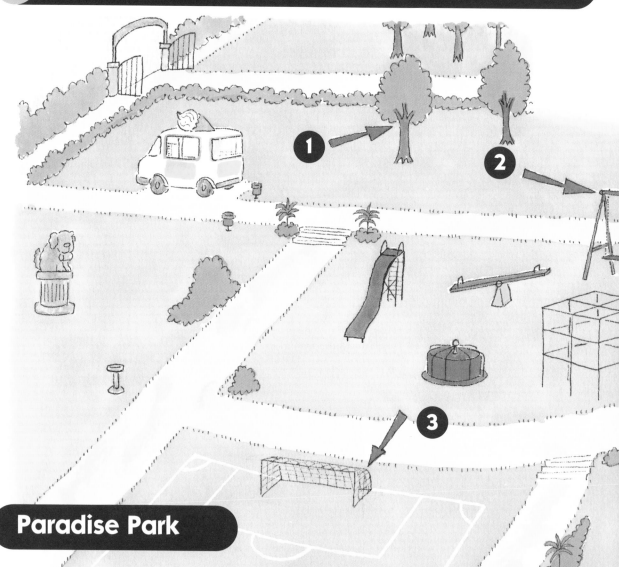

Paradise Park

1 Look at the picture map.

Talk with a partner. What does each arrow point to? Write a label for each one.

What would you like to do in Paradise Park?

2 Look at the map.

Think of a park you know or would like to visit.

Draw and label a map of it.

3 Write two sentences about what you can do in your park.

Dog Star

Spud and Jack were mates. They did everything together. If Spud liked something, his tail pointed. When Spud found a skateboard in the shed, Jack got it out. He painted silver and red stars on it.

While it was drying, Jack took Spud for a walk in the park. Uh oh! The big boys were there, kicking a football.

"What a funny looking dog!" cried Bob.

"That's not a dog. That's a bath mat!" said Nick. He had a mean laugh.

So Jack and Spud walked home fast.

Next day, the paint on the skateboard was dry. First of all, Jack skated up and down the lane. Then he did spins and jumps. Meanwhile, Spud's tail pointed. He wanted a go. Jack put the board down. Then he put Spud on top of it.

"Stay," said Jack. He put his foot on the back of the board and pushed. Spud's ears flicked up. Soon he could skate all the way to the end of the lane, while Jack ran alongside.

"Smart dog!" said Jack.

Before he took Spud to the park, Jack made a helmet for him out of an ice-cream tub. Then off they went to the skateboard ramp. Spud stayed on the board as it swished from side to side on the ramp.

"We should go on TV!" Jack said. But then – uh oh! – here came the big boys. Spud's ears stood stiff.

Bob pointed. "Hey, that's the dog we saw before!" he said. "He's on a skateboard. Do you think he can ride it?"

"Ha!" said Nick. "If he could, he'd be a dog star!" He had a mean laugh.

Then, Spud growled. He had a mean growl.

Nick gave Spud a hard push and grabbed the board.

Next thing, Spud grabbed him! He sank his teeth into Nick's shorts. *Rip*!

"My shorts!" Nick yelled.

"Nick," said Bob, "your bottom's showing." He laughed.

After that, Nick put his hands over his bottom and ran.

"He's smart, your dog," said Bob to Jack. Uh oh! This was one of the big boys!

"Yes," said Jack. "He can skate."

And Bob just asked, "Can I watch him?"

At last, Spud's tail pointed. His nose pointed. His ears flew out behind. At last, he was a dog star.

From *Dog Star* by Janeen Brian

1 Read **copymaster** 1. Then underline the words which tell you **when** things happen.

2 Read the last part of the story again.

Write a list of the words that tell you **when** things happen.

Bob pointed. "Hey, that's the dog we saw before!" he said. "He's on a skateboard. Do you think he can ride it?"

"Ha!" said Nick. "If he could, he'd be a dog star!" He had a mean laugh.

Then, Spud growled. He had a mean growl.

Nick gave Spud a hard push and grabbed the board.

Next thing, Spud grabbed him! He sank his teeth into Nick's shorts. *Rip!*

"My shorts!" Nick yelled.

"Nick," said Bob, "your bottom's showing." He laughed.

After that, Nick put his hands over his bottom and ran.

"He's smart, your dog," said Bob to Jack. Uh oh! This was one of the big boys!

"Yes," said Jack. "He can skate."

And Bob just asked, "Can I watch him?"

At last, Spud's tail pointed. His nose pointed. His ears flew out behind. At last, he was a dog star.

From *Dog Star* by Janeen Brian

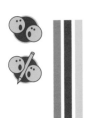

3 Look at the pictures and tell the story.

Write a sentence for each picture.

Use these words to begin your sentences.

Word bank

One day	Then
Next	In the end
But then	

1 Look at the sections of the picture of the park. Talk about a story that might start there.

2 Use **copymaster** 2 to help you plan your story.

3 Plan a story that takes place in Paradise Park.

Think about these questions when you plan the events and write out your answers as notes.

Event 1 How did it start?

Event 2 What happened?

Event 3 Did things get worse?

Event 4 How was it sorted out?
Did somebody help?

Event 5 How did it end?

NOW YOU ARE READY TO

draft your text ▶ revise and edit your text ▶ publish your text

ADDITIONAL SESSION

Writing a poem

1 Talk about the best, worst or funniest thing to do in the park. Now use **copymaster 3** to write your own park poem.

2 Write this poem frame.

Use it to write your own poem about people in the park.

> People in the park
> People in the park
>
> _____ people
> _____ people
> _____ing _____
> _____ing _____

3 Write your own poem.

Use one of the poems on **poster 5** to help you.

How to play hide and seek

What you need

3 or more people to play

a large space with places to hide

What you have to do

1 Choose one person to be 'it'.

2 Find a good place to hide while 'it' counts to 100.

3 Keep very quiet when 'it' starts looking.

4 Come out when 'it' finds you.

5 Start the game again. The person who was found last is 'it'.

1 Cut out the sentences on **copymaster** 4.

Match each sentence to one of these photographs. Number each sentence.

2 Look at these pictures. Can you put them in the right order?

Now tell a partner how to make a sandwich. Write an instruction for the first picture.

  3 Now talk about and write a 'What you need' list for making a sandwich.

 4 With a partner, choose one picture.

Can you give instructions for the activity?

a

b

c

1 Look at these pictures.

Talk about what you have to do.

Fill in the missing words on **copymaster 5**.

How to plant a conker

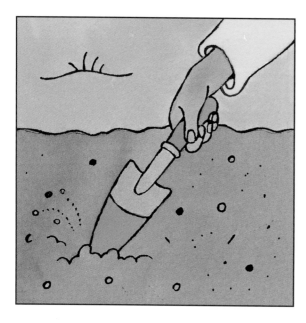

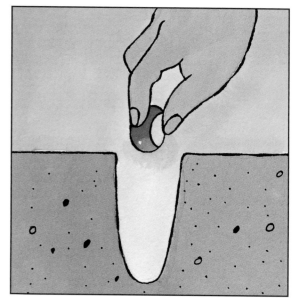

2 Look at these pictures.

Talk about what you have to do.

Fill in the missing words on **copymaster 6**.

How to play conkers

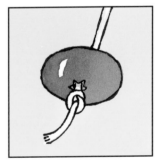

Read these instructions.

How to make a kite

What you need

one long stick (about 1 metre)

one shorter stick (about 50 cm)

ball of string

strong paper

scissors and glue

ribbon

What you have to do

1 Make a cross with the two sticks.

2 Tie the two sticks together with string.

3 Cut a small notch at the ends of both sticks.

4 Cut a long piece of string and stretch it around the kite frame.

5 Place the paper over the frame and cut around it.

6 Glue the paper to the frame.

7 Tie on a long length of string.

8 Make a tail by tying a ribbon to the bottom of the frame.

1 Start at step 2 and match each diagram to one of the steps. Then draw a diagram for step 1.

2 Match each diagram to one of the steps.

Then draw your own diagrams for step 1 and step 8.

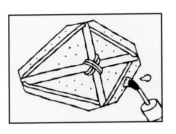 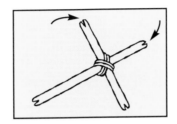 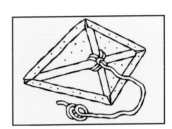

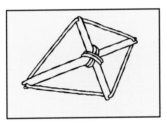 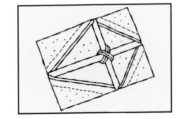 

 3 Use **copymaster 7**. Match the instructions to the diagrams and write the missing instructions.

 4 With a partner, talk about how to play one of these games.

Draw a diagram to make your instructions clearer.

football   noughts and crosses   rounders

NOW YOU ARE READY TO

plan your text ▶ draft your text ▶ revise and edit your text ▶ publish your text

Alligator

If you want to see an alligator
You must go down to the muddy slushy end
Of the old Caroony River

I know an alligator
Who's living down there
She's a-big. She's a-mean. She's a-wild.
She's a-fierce.

But if you really want to see an alligator
You must go down to the muddy slushy end
Of the old Caroony River

Go down gently to that river and say
"Alligator Mama
Alligator Mama
Alligator Mamaaaaaaaa"

And up she'll rise

But don't stick around
RUN FOR YOUR LIFE

by Grace Nichols

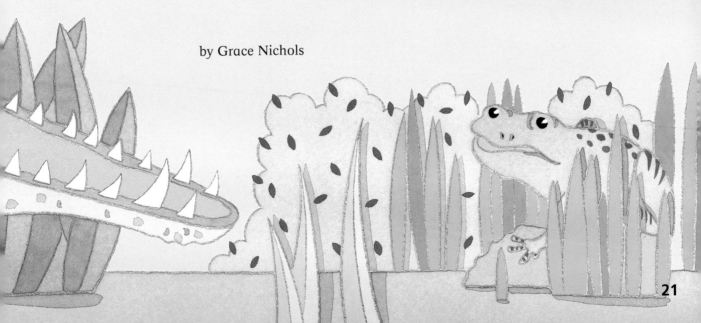

1 Look at these fierce creatures.

Choose one and talk about it with a partner.

- What is it like?
- How does it move?
- Where does it live?

Word bank
What it looks like
sly   fierce   savage scaly   powerful

2 Write some words to describe what your creature looks like.

 3 Write some words to describe where your creature lives and what it looks like.

 4 Write some words to describe where your creature lives and how it moves.

Word bank

How it moves

wriggle   hover
slither   sway   prowl
lurk   swoop   pounce
creep   glide

Where it lives

grassy plain
stinking swamp
baking desert

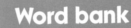

23

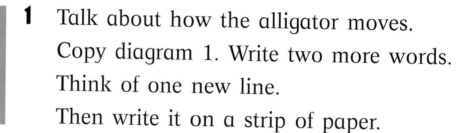

Read the poem on pages 20–21.

1 Talk about how the alligator moves.
Copy diagram 1. Write two more words.
Think of one new line.

Then write it on a strip of paper.

2 Copy diagrams 1 and 2. Write two new words for each.

Think of two new lines:
- one about how the alligator moves;
- one about what its jaws are like.

Write them on a strip of paper.

3 Copy diagrams 1, 2 and 3. Write two new words for each.

Think of three new lines:
- one about how the alligator moves;
- one about what its jaws are like;
- one about its eyes.

Write them on a strip of paper.

Now read the poem again with your line(s) added.

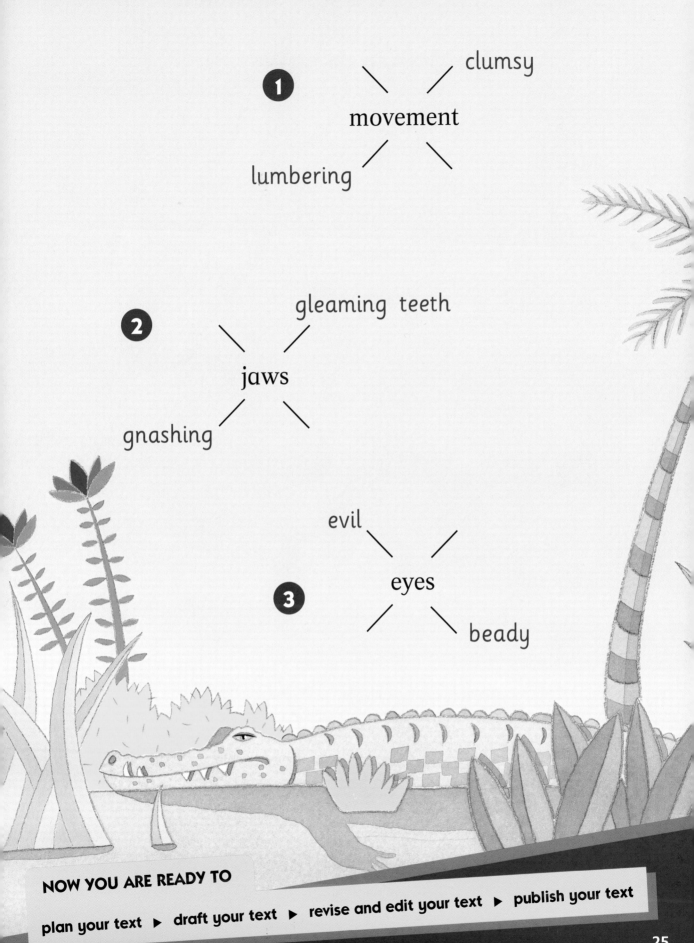

1

clumsy

movement

lumbering

2

gleaming teeth

jaws

gnashing

3

evil

eyes

beady

NOW YOU ARE READY TO

plan your text ▶ draft your text ▶ revise and edit your text ▶ publish your text

Story settings

1 Write about being inside the elephant.

Use **copymaster 10** to help you.

Word bank

swishing	bones
people	squelching
porridge	animals
dancing	gurgling

2 Imagine you are inside the elephant's stomach.

What can you see, smell, touch and hear?

Write four sentences.

Look at the word bank for some ideas.

Think of some more words of your own.

Start your sentences like this. Copy these into your book.

I can see . . .

I can smell . . .

I can touch . . .

I can hear . . .

1 Talk about what the enormous one-tusked elephant is like. Here are some words to help you.

Word bank

one tusk   fierce   angry
bad-tempered

Make a 'Wanted' poster. Use **copymaster 11** to help you.

2 Talk about how the elephant would describe Unanana. Here are some words to help you.

Word bank		
brave	bossy	noisy
fearless	clever	resourceful

Make a 'Wanted' poster.

Warn the other animals what she is like.

WANTED

Name: _____

Wanted because _____

_____

What she looks like: _____

_____

_____ is very _____
(name)

and _____

_____

4 How to write

an explanation

A good way to trap a fierce creature

1   **2**

Fierce creatures can be dangerous because they have sharp teeth and might attack you. If there is one in your garden, you could use a giant vacuum cleaner to trap it. This is how the trap works.

First, the creature smells food on the ground. It eats it. Then, it follows a trail of food to a dish. When it gets near the dish it steps on an electric switch. This switch turns on a giant vacuum cleaner.

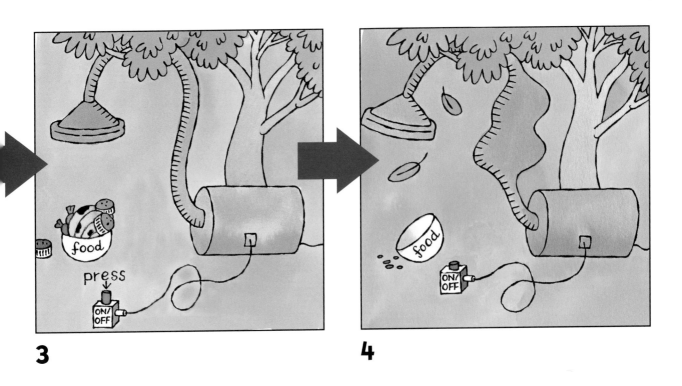

3   **4**

Because the fierce creature is standing just under the nozzle, it is sucked up into the hose. Next, it is sucked right into the vacuum cleaner.

Finally, the fierce creature is taken back to the wild.

This trap always works because fierce creatures are always hungry. They will always follow the food. Also they do not understand how vacuum cleaners work. So they will not know they are being trapped.

1 Looking at an explanation

1 Read these questions. Talk about the answers with a partner.

> **1** Why can fierce creatures be dangerous?
>
> **2** Why does the fierce creature get sucked up the hose?
>
> **3** Why does the fierce creature trap always work?
>
> **4** Why does the trap need a switch?
>
> **5** Why do you need a giant vacuum cleaner?

Now use **copymaster 12**.

Put the number of the right question next to each answer.

2 Cut out the diagrams on **copymaster 12**.

Put them in the right order. Write a title.

Tell your partner how the trap works.

3 Read the explanation of an elephant trap on page 33.

Talk about how it works.

Then answer the questions on page 34.

One way to trap an elephant

Elephants can be a problem because they eat too many fresh green leaves. If you had one in your garden, you could catch it with this trap. Here is how it works.

First, the elephant finds fresh leaves on the ground. Because elephants are greedy, it will stop and eat them.

As soon as you see the elephant eating, you turn the handle quickly. This makes the drum go round. The rope unwinds, so the grabber comes down and grabs the elephant.

Next, the elephant jumps up and down because it is cross. This makes the grabber close, so that the elephant is trapped. Then you turn the handle the other way.

The grabber moves up because the rope winds round the drum again. Finally, the elephant is up in the air and can be dropped into a big box.

1　　　**2**　　　**3**　　　**4**

Write answers to these questions.

1 Why are elephants a problem?
Because _____

2 Why does the elephant eat the leaves?
Because _____

3 Why do you turn the handle and unwind the rope?
So that _____

4 Why does the elephant jump up and down?
Because _____

5 Why does the grabber close?
So that _____

4 Write another question for your partner about the elephant trap.

Hint!

Who?
What?
Why?
When?
Where?
How?

HOME

1   Look at the diagrams. They show how baby alligators are born.

Explain this to a partner.

Then look at the questions on page 36.

How baby alligators are born

female makes nest

lays 40–50 eggs

guards the nest

eggs begin to hatch and female uncovers them

35

III Talk about answers to these questions.

> **1** How does the alligator make its nest?
>
> **2** How many eggs does she lay?
>
> **3** Why does the alligator cover up the eggs?
>
> **4** Why does she guard the nest?
>
> **5** Why does she uncover the eggs?

 2 Write a caption for diagram 6.

Write it down in your book.

3 Write captions for diagrams 3 and 6.

Write them down in your book.

4 Write captions for diagrams 3, 6 and 7.

Write them down in your book.

NOW YOU ARE READY TO

plan your text ▶ draft your text ▶ revise and edit your text ▶ publish your text

Making a class dictionary

1 Talk about these animals. Match each one with the right definition.

lion   tarantula   shark   tiger   wolf

a mammal like a big dog, that hunts in packs

a dangerous, striped cat that lives in India

a fierce and powerful fish

a big, fierce cat; the male has a shaggy mane

a big, hairy, poisonous spider

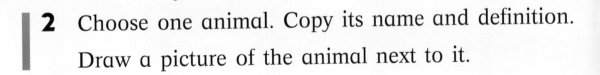

2 Choose one animal. Copy its name and definition. Draw a picture of the animal next to it.

3 Write down these names in alphabetical order.

alligator   rhinoceros   python
panther   sting-ray

4 Choose two animals. Write definitions for them.

5 Choose four animals. Write definitions for them.

Deadly Friend

"Children, meet Adam Starbright!"

The children gawped and giggled as their teacher frowned disapprovingly at their bad manners.

Adam Starbright stood stiffly at Mrs Walker's side. He was a bit like a dummy standing in the window of a clothing store. His face was as still as plastic and his eyes were the colour of water. His clothes were odd too. They were similar to the grey and maroon uniform they all wore, yet somehow different. They were smooth and tight-fitting, as though his body had been poured into them.

Adam stared at Mohun. The new boy's eyes gazed steadily into his without blinking. Mohun stared back. He couldn't help it. It was as if Adam's gaze was a trap which had caught him and wouldn't let him go.

"Now then everybody, get out your English notebooks. I want you to write about your best friend."

There was a rattle of drawers opening, as everyone pulled out exercise books and snatched up pencils. Out of the corner of his eye, Mohun had the impression that Adam didn't open his drawer. The boy's hand went straight through the table top, as if it were water, and came out holding his book. Then in strange, printy handwriting, moving to the right and back again like a computer printout, Adam wrote, "My best friend is Mohun."

From *Deadly Friend* by Jamila Gavin

1 Look at the pictures. With a partner choose one of the aliens and talk about what it looks like, what it is wearing and how it moves. Write some words to describe it.

2 Look at the pictures. With a partner talk about what the aliens look like, what they are wearing and how they move. Write some words to describe them.

3 Now imagine your own alien.

 Copy the chart and write words to describe it.

What it looks like	What it wears	How it moves

4 Now draw your own alien.

Write labels to show its special features.

2 Story settings

1 Look at the picture.

Then talk about it with a partner.

What can you see?

What can you hear?

Fill in **copymaster 15**.

2 Choose two pictures and talk about them with a partner.

What can you see in each picture?

What can you hear?

Write about both settings on **copymaster 15**.

3 Talk about all three pictures with a partner.

What can you see in each picture?

What can you hear?

Write about all three settings on **copymaster 15**.

1 Look at the pictures. Talk about the story of Adam Starbright.

How is the ending different?

 Write a sentence for the last picture.

2 Look at the pictures for the story of Adam Starbright.

Write one sentence about each picture.

Watch out! The ending is different!

3 Here are two more different endings to the story.

Write one sentence about each picture.

Talk about which ending you like best.

1 Use **copymaster 16**. Talk about what Simon and Mohun might be saying. Fill in the speech bubbles.

2 Look at the picture.
What does Mohun say? What does Adam say?
Talk about what Simon might say.
Now fill in **copymaster 17**.

3 Talk about this picture.

Imagine Simon and Mohun are talking about Adam.

What do you think they say?

Write a conversation between them. You can copy this frame and use it to help you.

Mohun and Simon got their skateboards. Simon turned to Mohun and asked him, "_____

_____

_____?"

  Mohun hesitated. "_____

_____,"

he answered.

NOW YOU ARE READY TO

plan your text ▶ draft your text ▶ revise and edit your text ▶ publish your text

The Alien Visitor

When the alien visitor
Visits our school,
Please be polite to him,
Don't play the fool.

His skin may be purple
Or orange or blue,
But you must not be rude,
Whatever you do.

He may have two heads
But you mustn't make fun.
Remember that two heads
Are better than one.

Quiet a moment!
I've just had a note.
It's written in alien.
It says, and I quote:

"BOING, YARP PALARVA
BEEP PLARGLE SPLING SPLOFF!"
He's seen our school photo –
It's frightened him off!

by Colin McNaughton

1 Use **copymaster 21** to write your own verse.

2 Talk about what the last two lines of this verse might be.

Then write out your own new verse 2.

> His skin may be purple
> Or orange or white
> But _____
>
> _____

Now make up some new nonsense words for the last verse.

Write out your own last verse.

> _____
>
> _____
>
> He's seen our school photo –
> It's frightened him off!

3 Finish this new verse.

> He may be enormous,
> He may be quite small,
> But _____
>
> _____

Writing jokes and tongue-twisters

1 Here are some lists of 'space' words.

Use one set to make a tongue-twister.

You can add one or two words that begin with another letter if you want.

Write out your tongue-twister and test it on a friend.

Saturn	space	spotting	
saw	silly	six	stars

Mars	monkey	missed	my
mouse	met	mean	more

pick	planet	pink	Pete's
please	pass	Pluto	plump

2 These jokes have got mixed up.

Sort them out.

Then write them out as a joke book for Adam Starbright.

A pale-ien.

What's an alien's favourite tea?

An aliiien.

What flowers grow on the other side of the moon?

An unidentified frying saucer.

What do you call a spaceship that goes too close to the sun?

Gravi-tea.

What do you call an ill alien?

Sunflowers.

What do you call an alien with three eyes?

 Now make up your own answer for this question:

What are an alien's favourite sweets?

Writing a book review

Copy this frame into your book or use **copymaster 22**.

Write your own book review.

Title: _____

Written by _____

Illustrated by _____

I like this story because _____
_____

The characters are _____
_____

The pictures are _____
_____

The most enjoyable part of the story is when _____
_____
_____

I think _____
would like this book.

Hint!

Tips on writing your book review

- Choose a story you know lots about.
- Think about which characters you like, and why.
- Think about which part you enjoyed most, and why.
- Did you like the ending of the story?
- Think about **why** you like this book.
- Think about who else would enjoy this book.

How to write

a non-chronological report

Mars – the red planet

Mars is the first **planet** beyond Earth. It looks red because the rocks and sand are red with dust. It is just over half the size of Earth.

Scientists can find out about Mars by sending robot explorers to take photographs. There is no life on Mars because it is too cold and too dry for anything to live there.

There are winds, frost, clouds and mist on Mars. It is much colder in the morning than in the middle of the day. When the Sun goes down, it gets cold again. A strong wind blows most of the time. Often there are dust storms that last for weeks.

Mars has many **volcanoes** and valleys. The rest of Mars is flat and made of sand and rocks – like a cold, stony desert.

Mars fact file

- Martian year = 687 Earth days
- Martian day = 24 hours and 37 minutes
- Temperature range = −140°C to 20°C
- Number of moons = 2
- Average distance from the Sun = 227 million kilometres

Glossary

planet
a large object in space that goes round a star

volcanoes
mountains with holes at the top which let out burning rocks and gases

1 Read the report about Mars.

With a partner, find:

- a technical word;
- a present tense verb;
- a fact.

Now write them down.

Mars – the red planet

Mars looks red because the rocks and sand are red. It is smaller than Earth.

There is no life on Mars. It is too cold and too dry for anything to live there.

There are winds, frost, clouds and mist on Mars. A strong wind blows most of the time.

Mars has many volcanoes and valleys.

Mars fact file

- Martian year = 687 Earth days
- Martian day = 24 hours and 37 minutes
- Number of moons = 2

2 Read the report about Saturn.

With a partner, find two:

- technical words;
- present tense verbs;
- facts.

Now write them down.

Saturn – the ringed planet

Saturn has many rings round it. It is the second biggest planet (Jupiter is the biggest). Seen through a telescope, Saturn is yellow in colour.

Saturn has 18 satellite moons. They are made of ice. The largest moon is called Titan.

Saturn's rings are made of chunks of rock and ice. They move quickly around the planet.

There are strong winds on Saturn and many clouds. There is a giant storm once every 30 years.

Saturn fact file

- Saturn's day = 10.25 Earth hours

- Saturn's year = 29.5 Earth years

- Distance from the Sun = 1.4 billion kilometres

1 Read the report on **copymaster 23**.

Write these headings above the right section.

What Mars looks like

The weather on Mars

Life on Mars

2 Use **copymaster 23** again.

Now write these sentences under the right headings.

Mars is much colder than Earth.

There are many valleys on the surface of Mars.

There is not enough air on Mars for plants or animals.

3 Use **copymaster 24**.

Write these headings above the right section.

Saturn's rings

Saturn's weather

Saturn's moons

4 Use **copymaster 24** again.

Write these sentences under the right headings.

There are more than 100,000 rings around Saturn.

Titan is the only one of Saturn's moons with its own atmosphere.

The wind on Saturn can blow at more than 1,800 kilometres per hour.

5 Think of a new heading for this section.

The inside part of Saturn is made of rock. Outside this there is a layer of liquid metal – this is surrounded by gases.

1 Read these sentences to your partner.

Which ones are right for a report? Write them down.

Earth's landscape

I like going to the beach.
There is sand on the beaches.
My uncle climbs mountains.

Earth's weather

I love splashing in puddles.
It is fun to play in the snow.
It is very hot in the desert.

2 Look at the pictures and talk about the weather on Earth.

What sort of sentences would you write in a report?

Write three sentences to go with the heading 'Earth's weather'.

Word bank			
snow	wind	storm	gale
rain	thunder	ice	lightning

3 Look at the pictures above and talk about the weather on Earth.

Then talk about human beings.

Write two sentences to go with the headings: 'Earth's weather' and 'Human beings'.

Hint!

1 Include facts.

2 Don't write about personal feelings.

3 Don't use 'I' or 'we'.

4 Use the present tense.

NOW YOU ARE READY TO

plan your text ▶ draft your text ▶ revise and edit your text ▶ publish your text

Making notes

1 Find the number facts in the report.

Then make notes on **copymaster 26**.

2 Work with a partner, using **copymaster 27**.

Note down the number facts in the report.

Then make notes about the landscape and the weather.

Use your notes to tell your partner about Earth.

Earth – the living planet

Earth is the third planet from the Sun. It is different from the other planets.

There is life on Earth. As far as we know, there is no life on any other planet. Millions of different plants and animals as well as humans live on Earth. They all need water. And a lot of Earth is covered with water. There are oceans and seas and rivers.

Some places are very dry, like the desert. Some places are very cold, like the Arctic. It is difficult for most animals and plants to live in these places. But many places, like hills, valleys, forests and open plains, are just right for them. Plants and animals need temperatures that are not too cold and not too hot. Temperatures can be as low as −80°C in Antarctica and as high as 57°C in Africa, but this is too much for most plants and animals.

The weather on Earth is different in different places. It also changes at different times of the year. There are storms and winds and rain and frost and sun and snow.

Earth has one moon. Each year is 365 days long and each day is 24 hours long.

PUBLISHED BY THE PRESS SYNDICATE OF THE UNIVERSITY OF CAMBRIDGE
The Pitt Building, Trumpington Street, Cambridge, United Kingdom

CAMBRIDGE UNIVERSITY PRESS
The Edinburgh Building, Cambridge CB2 2RU, UK
40 West 20th Street, New York, NY 10011-4211, USA
477 Williamstown Road, Port Melbourne, VIC 3207, Australia
Ruiz de Alarcón 13, 28014 Madrid, Spain
Dock House, The Waterfront, Cape Town 8001, South Africa

http://www.cambridge.org

First published 2002

Printed in the United Kingdom at the University Press, Cambridge

Typeface Concorde Infant and Edukabel   *System* QuarkXPress®

A catalogue record for this book is available from the British Library

Library of Congress Cataloguing in Publication data

ISBN 0 521 75197 7

Design by Angela Ashton and Karen Thomas
Picture Research by Angela Ashton and Karen Thomas
Artwork chosen by Angela Ashton and Karen Thomas
Illustrations by Beccy Blake, Sally Kindberg, Rachel Merriman/Heather Richards,
Ian Newsham/Heather Richards, Sami Sweeten/Heather Richards, Amanda Wood/
Linda Rogers Associates
Photography by John Walmsey www.educationphotos.co.uk, pages 14, 15, 18, 42, 43, 58 left
and 61 bottom

We are grateful to the following for permission to reproduce text extracts:
Dog Star © Janeen Brian, reproduced by permission of Southwood Books Ltd; 'The Hardest
Thing to do in the World' by Michael Rosen, text © Michael Rosen, from *Don't Put Mustard in the
Custard* published by Scholastic, 1996; *Alligator* © Grace Nichols, 1988, reproduced with permission
of Curtis Brown Ltd, London, on behalf of Grace Nichols; *Deadly Friend* copyright Jamilia Gavin,
publisher Egmont Books Ltd, London; 'The Alien Visitor' by Colin McNaughton from *Making
Friends with Frankenstein* © 1993, 2000 Colin McNaughton, reproduced by permission of the
publisher, Walker Books Limited; 'Unanana and the Enormous One-Tusked Elephant' by Margaret
Mayo from *The Orchard Book of Magical Tales* by Margaret Mayo, first published in the UK by
Orchard Books in 1993, a division of the Watts Publishing Group Limited, London.

We are grateful to the following for permission to reproduce photographs and illustrations:
Illustration from *Cloudland* by John Burningham published by Jonathan Cape. Used by permission
of The Random House Group Limited; Cover illustration from *Katie Morag Delivers the Mail* by
Mairi Hedderwick published by Red Fox. Used by permission of The Random House Group Limited;
Cover illustration from *Amazing Grace* by Mary Hoffman illustrated by Caroline Binch, published
by Frances Lincoln Ltd, © 1991. Reproduced by permission of Frances Lincoln Ltd, London; Cover
illustration from *The Hundred-Mile-An-Hour Dog* by Jeremy Strong, published by Viking, 1996, text
© Jeremy Strong 1996, Illustrations © Nick Sharratt 1996.

Every effort has been made to trace all copyright holders. If there are any outstanding copyright
issues if which we are unaware, please contact Cambridge University Press.